Wild Friends

Annette Swart

Copyright © 2015 Annette Swart. All rights reserved.

ISBN
978-1-4828-0627-4 (sc)
978-1-4828-0626-7 (e)

All rights reserved. No part of this book may be used or reproduced by any means, graphic, electronic, or mechanical, including photocopying, recording, taping or by any information storage retrieval system without the written permission of the publisher except in the case of brief quotations embodied in critical articles and reviews.

Because of the dynamic nature of the Internet, any web addresses or links contained in this book may have changed since publication and may no longer be valid. The views expressed in this work are solely those of the author and do not necessarily reflect the views of the publisher, and the publisher hereby disclaims any responsibility for them.

Print information available on the last page.

To order additional copies of this book, contact
Toll Free 0800 990 914 (South Africa)
+44 20 3014 3997 (outside South Africa)
orders.africa@partridgepublishing.com

www.partridgepublishing.com/africa

04/16/2015

PARTRIDGE
A Penguin Random House Company

For Ben

Giraffe is a wild animal who lives in the bush.
He is very tall with brown spots.

Zebra is also a wild animal. He has a beautiful black and white striped coat. Zebra lives in the bush with Giraffe.

Giraffe and Zebra look very different to each other yet they are best friends.

They stroll in the bush and eat together. Zebra grazes the grass and Giraffe eats the juicy leaves off the top of the tree.

One day, Giraffe and Zebra were at their favourite waterhole. Giraffe was drinking while Zebra was looking out for any danger.

Monkey was also on the lookout for danger!

Both Zebra and Giraffe got a terrible fright when they heard Monkey shout . . .

"Danger! Run!"

Lion licked his lips as he chased the two terrified friends.

Giraffe and Zebra ran and ran as fast as they could. They had to get far away from Lion!

Lion was still running at high speed when suddenly, banana peels landed on his head and over his eyes!

CRASH! OUCH!

Sore and sorry for himself, Lion limped slowly back to the bush.

The lovebirds flew off to find Giraffe and Zebra, to tell them that brave Monkey had chased Lion away.

Happy and feeling safe together! Wild friends forever and ever!

Lightning Source UK Ltd.
Milton Keynes UK
UKOW07f0651270515

252360UK00009B/39/P